The Lonely Shade

by

Mary B. Lyons

A collection of original and universally appealing poems for funerals and the comfort of the bereaved.
There is a companion CD entitled
The Lonely Shade – CD

About the Author

Mary B. Lyons, an established writer in several genres, was born in Surrey, England and has been writing poetry since the age of eight years. *The Lonely Shade* is her second publication. During her Samaritan training Mary gained an insight into grief and bereavement which is reflected in the sensitively composed poems of *The Lonely Shade*. This booklet and companion CD offer comfort, understanding and hope.

Contents

FOR BEREAVED PEOPLE EVERYWHERE

Letting go

I'm letting you go to a better place,
Though hard, and I'll miss your gentle face,
But the moment's right to say "Goodbye",
To let the teardrops flow, and sigh,
For our time together is no more
And I say "Farewell", of that I'm sure.
The hours we shared, so edged with laughter,
Will stay with me forever after,
Echoes cascading down the years,
Drying away today's sad tears.
I will remember. I'll never forget
That to you I owe the ultimate debt
For support and kindness, wisdom too,
That flowed from you to see me through.
So thank you for this peaceful end
To the life of my dearest friend.

A Sudden Storm

A sudden storm engulfed your life
And swept your soul away.
The wind of change relentlessly
Scattered petalled flowers.
One moment you were with us,
But at the break of day,
We found that you had slipped this world
Like fleeting April showers.

The autumn leaves swirled 'round the place.
They rattled on the ground.
Winter's icy blast took hold
And grasped the frozen lands.
The bitter cold encircled all
In nature to be found
But in the darkness came the hope
Of silent helping hands.

The strength to deal with sorrow
Reaches all who dare to ask.
No matter how intense the depth
And power of the pain,
Courage flows like healing balm
To ease the saddest task
And raises us 'til we may seize
The chance to live again.

An Empty Place

There's an empty place in my arms,
For you are no longer there.
There's a vacant space at the table
And nobody sits in your chair.
Your coat still hangs in the hall.
Your shoes sit sad on the rack.
The dog searches for you in vain.
He knows you will never come back.

The laughter has gone from the house.
The curtains drape limp at the frame,
And nobody calls back to me
When I huskily whisper your name.
The postman delivers your mail
And the letters pile up on the side
Near the picture of us on the day
We married, a young groom and bride.

Nobody warned me the end
Would be sudden and cruel and so sad
That the desperate panic and pain
Would be so incredibly bad.
Please tell me before my heart breaks
That this feeling of loss will diminish,
That time will bring ease to the ache
That promises never to finish.

Don’t Weep for Me

Don’t weep for me
For I am going to another place
Where you cannot follow, for now,
But I will wait for you,
Silent in the shadows,
Playful in the sunlight,
Dancing on the water.
My spirit will be always with you,
So talk with me and walk with me
In the places we both shared,
Knowing that this separation is not forever
And one day we will meet again,
Reunited in our love.

Eternal Rest

Death is the beginning of
  A time we've never known
When thoughts of life and living from
  The world have gently flown,
A door that's flung wide open just
  To let the starlight in.
The past is but a closing book.
  Let new life begin!

Forget the pain and sorrow, all
  The heartache, dread and need.
With both hands take the treasure up,
  On which the soul can feed.
Abandon thoughts of darkest fear.
  Clasp eternal light.
Grasp the hand of hope now as
  It leads you from the night.

We who are remaining and
  Do not this journey make,
Must say farewell to you now
  And other by-ways take,
For life is just a floating dream,
  A challenge and a test
That copes with stress and sorrow 'til
  It seeks eternal rest.

Dear Friend

Dear Friend,
I see you slip into another land.
My words of comfort poured like silver sand,
Skim past your ears, your paling, old eyes and
Hover in the space between we two.
The years stretch back. We saw them sweetly
through.
We shared the dazzling sun and midnight blue.

Dear Friend,
Your shifting consciousness of drifting days,
Of time and distance, all become a haze.
You clutch at me to guide you through the ways,
The convoluted path that lies ahead.
One day soon I know your empty bed
Will tell me that the life we shared is dead.

Dear Friend,
It's desperate and so hard to let you go,
To see your fire turn to an ember glow,
To watch the final curtain of the show,
To see you close the door on this last class,
Knowing that our special time must pass
And soon you will be ash on blossomed grass.

Dear Friend,
One day soon I know alone I'll be,
And from your agèd frame you will be free.
I will forget these trying times and see
You, and how we vowed our life to spend,
Two lonely souls who love to each did lend,
And not recall this sad and bitter end.

Dear Friend,
Although your faculties now seem to fade
And all our tunes are well and truly played,
And lifestyle finally shifts from light to shade,
There is one thing you really have to know:
The love we shared shone like the driven snow
And leaves behind a splendid after-glow.

A Big Question

Will dancing, always joyous to my soul,
Remind me ever of your tender touch?
Can I waltz or glide a ballroom floor
Without a thought of you I loved so much?

Will music, happy heaven to my heart
Remind me of our own romantic themes?
Can I sing or hum a tune that we both knew
Without a thought of you within my dreams?

Will words, that gift we both hold oh so dear,
Remind me ever of your canny guile?
Can I say verse or read your letters too
Without a thought of you and your shy smile?

Will skies or fields or autumn's rustling leaves
Remind me always of a walk we shared?
Can I breathe air, live life or face the hours
Without a thought of you for whom I cared?

Will I, one day, pick up my shredded soul,
Recalling special moments, fun or tragic
To fumble forward, onward with my life
Knowing what we had was priceless magic!

A Tiny Star

You were lent to us for such a little while,
And left so soon before you learned to smile.
We'd hardly time to even choose your name.
What talents lay within your tiny frame,
Never to blossom or see the light of day?
We lost them all when you went on your way.
Compassion for our sorrow's all around.
You said "Farewell" without the slightest sound,
Quietly slipping off to another place,
With a peaceful, silent shadow on your face.

Irreplaceable, tiny little mite,
You struggled so for life with such a fight,
And lost the battle without a single cry,
While we watched you vainly, sitting by,
Hour upon hour, hoping patiently,
But you slept and crept into eternity.
For the rest of time your absence will be clear,
Compounded by events from year to year,
As we must learn to live with searing grief
For our tiny star whose sparkle was so brief.

The River of Life

From source to sea the river flows,
Sparkling, dancing, slow or deep.
Its convoluted course it charts,
Relentless as you softly sleep.
What joy you found in sporting there,
Amid the fields and larks on high!
How lovely were the caddis flies,
You made to tempt the fish come by!

It takes all sorts to make a world.
Nature varies her design.
We'll think of you by dawn's first light,
Poised and still with rod and line,
To harvest glistening fish with eyes,
That look and gleam to skies above.
May eternity be this for you,
A purest, never-ending love.

The Lonely Shade

There are some deaths in private style,
Not publicised but quiet and small,
Personal and deeply sad,
Not discussed or seen at all.
No funeral flowers or mourners there
To grieve the tiny being lost
That went away in privacy
The path from life to death so crossed.
"Miscarriage" happens to so many.
"Forget it dear and try again!"
Who understands the desolation,
Disappointment, pointless pain?

Other children come along.
The world thinks "Past is really past".
Bereavement lasts a lifetime though.
The loss is there from first to last.
What might have been has gone for good,
A future blank, devoid of joy.
Every mother feels the loss
Of embryonic girl or boy.
Down the decades unsung songs,
Memories that were not made.
All of our lost babies lie
In bereavement's lonely shade.

Below Par

It's a beautiful day on the golf course.
There's not a sound to be heard
But a zephyr-like breeze
As it teases the trees
And competes with the song of a bird.

You tee off with utter perfection.
Your swing is a joy to the eyes.
The ball's splendid in flight
But veers to the right
And gives you a lovely surprise.

It nestles up close to the target,
The best that it ever has been.
You feel so inspired,
A putt is required,
As you stand, full of hope, on the green.

You take a look in your golf bag.
You rummage around like a mole.
With encouraging mutter,
You take out a putter
To sink the ball in the hole.

So the morning progresses.
You've never encountered such play.
You don't want to hunker
Down in the bunker
And fortune smiles sweetly today.

At the eighteenth your card is a picture,
A symphony full of low scores.
You're well below par
And feel like a star.
"I'll have a double. What's yours?"

That's how you'll be remembered
Every bright, sunny day,
As you just follow through
On a green fresh with dew.
We'll pretend that you've not gone away.

The Gift

There is a special time and place
For every living thing:
The bloom of flowers, the fleeting hours

And all the birds that sing.
For every season there's a proper,
Passing human phase:
Rites of passage, nights of darkness,
Sunny, halcyon days.

Buds and blossoms, chased by zephyrs,
Autumn's vibrant leaves,
Birth and marriage, loss, bereavement;

Everybody grieves.
From spring's rejoicing, gliding through
To summer's sweet content,
All human souls this glorious
Tapestry are lent.

She made a family, raised them all
With love throughout the years,
A woman for each season, so

Brush away your tears!
A gift we'll all remember in
Winter's darkest hour,
A gift we must return now,
An everlasting flower.

The Distant Land

No one knows the path that may
Have led you to this place,
What went on behind those eyes
And smiling, patient face.
No one knows the darkness that
You battled with so long.
No one knows the moment when
You chose to end the song.

We only know we love you and
Our lives are sad, bereft.
If only you had called us just
Before you quietly left.
Couldn't we have helped you to
Avoid this final scene?
Forever we'll be tortured by
The things that might have been.

Whatever lies beyond this time,
We do not understand,
But travel now with peaceful heart
Into the distant land,
While we caress the golden hours
Of all that your life meant
And never cease to thank the stars
That you, to us, were lent.

The Stony Path

We watched you walk along the lonesome,
Stony path of pain,
Fearing that the life you knew
Would never come again.
We saw you suffer daily in a
Place that was your own.
With aching hearts we knew you'd go
The way that you'd been shown.
Our helplessness was pitiful,
Your bravery so great
As you gave your weary body to
The welcome arms of fate.
You slipped away so gently like
A blossom on the tide,
With loved ones gathered 'round you and
Mercy at your side.
Every life is precious, be it
Present, future, past
But we must now be grateful that
You've found your peace at last.

Dance with Me

Come dance with me
Through eternity!
We'll waltz 'til the end of time,
With feet as light
As a summer night
And the music so sublime.
With your chiffon gown
And a golden crown
We will fly over hill and dale.
We will drift and sway
'Til the break of day
When the moon grows ever pale.

What's that you say?
You must go away,
No more to dance on dew?
As you fade to mist,
By the morning kissed,
How I long so to follow you.
Though our time is past
And it went so fast
In our bevy of human schemes,
Until we meet
At destiny's feet,
I'll dance with you in my dreams.

Eight Words

Nothing can prepare you for
The shock of sudden death,
How to deal with knowing that
The loved one's final breath
Has now been drawn, and you must face
The future full of fears.
Give into your sorrow and
Never mind the tears,
For every single soul on Earth
Must be where you now stand,
Desolate and doubting with
Sad flowers in your hand.
These eight words will help you
As the months and years tick past.
Look back, then remember how
You coped and won at last!

Loss is such a little word
For wholesale devastation,
Disbelief, - a puzzling feeling
Mixed with irritation,
Grief, - a puny way to say
"massive desecration"
And *Anger* understands the rage
That comes from dreadful pain.
From *Sadness* flows acceptance of
The things you cannot fight,
While *Resolution* helps you through
The small hours of the night.
Remembrance will, in time, be good
But always keep in sight,
That one day you will face the sun
And gladly *Smile* again.

Sad Song

For the first time in ages I play my guitar.
I strum in the twilight and sing "la la la"
To cheer myself up.
My heart sings with the strings
As they vibrate and twang,
Recalling a song that the two of us sang,
Long ago, sweet and low.
I won't play it again. It brings back such pain.

The Most Important View

We enter this world alone
And we leave it on our own.
How we are remembered
Depends on many things.
Those who are remaining
May think of us complaining.
Those of similar mind
May speak of us as kind.
No matter what they say,
On this, the farewell day,
The most important view
Is what *you* thought of *you*.

The Bell's Last Chime

At this annual freezing season,
Sorrow is our only reason
To be full of grief.
As we trudge through snowfall sadly,
Others pass us by so gladly,
Full of disbelief.

We know that in each winter's thrall,
We will remember, one and all,
On such a frosty day,
While snow lay deep upon the ground,
Muffling all of nature's sound,
You chose to go away.

Parcels posted, sweetmeats made,
Tables for the feasting laid.
Décor glittered so,
But in your bed with linen white
You gently drifted through the night.
It was time to go.

We said "Goodbye" and wept our tears
Knowing that, in future years
We would recall these hours.
While all around sought to rejoice,
We knew you had no other choice,
Like autumn's final flowers.

Would that you had chosen, dear,
Some other month within the year,
Another point in time,
To leave this weary, earthly place,
Serene at last your tranquil face,
Called by the bell's last chime.

Farewell to Chains

Fling wide the windows of the mind!
Draw back the drapes of doom!
Let enter flooding rays of sun
To bathe the inner room!

Say farewell to darkened days,
To blinkered duty hollow!
Fill the soul with sheer delight
And in pleasure wallow!

Life is short and old age long.
The cricket's on the hearth.
We may die at any time,
On stairs, on street, in bath.

To wake each day with leaden heart
Is not what life is for.
So cut the chains and use your brains!
Open now the door!

As some will leave the portal's shade,
Others will arrive.
The changing tapestry of time
Helps us to survive.

Greet with peace each one who calls
To offer friendship's dove.
Welcome them with open arms
Which speak of joy and love.

The Velvet Glove

Death comes stealing quietly in
The softest velvet glove,
As gentle as the feathers on
A snow-white, resting dove,
As peaceful as the tide as
It turns to ebb away,
As final as the sunset at
The close of perfect day.

Where once the cherished footsteps fell
To lighten winter's gloom,
No more the face we loved so much
Illuminates the room.
Beloved voice is heard no more,
The laughter ever lost,
Familiar roads and by-ways bare,
No longer to be crossed.

Footsteps in the sands of time,
Imprints cast in air,
The memories will linger for
As long as we all care.
The picture of our dear one,
Forever in our mind,
Wise and good and clever but
Most of all just kind.

The Edge

As dawn came up along the seaside bay
I watched the fishing boats go on their way.
The morning mist proclaimed a brand new day.
My heart stood still.

The softly creeping waves ran up the strand
To rocks just out of reach on yielding sand
Where little pools of salt-life dabbled, and
My heart stood still.

On craggy cliffs we lingered side by side.
The wheeling, shrieking gulls around us cried
And, deep below, the ever turning tide.
My heart stood still.

Like clinging gulls on crumbling cliff-top ledge,
Grab onto life and give it one proud pledge:
To hold on fast when there you see the edge,
Though your heart stands still.

For all the birds and waves and rolling mist
Are part of one great plan we can't resist,
Which puts us in our place when first we're kissed
And our hearts stand still.

Roulette

You are not here.
We assemble to bid you farewell
But you have already gone.
It is a sombre party
Where the principal guest
Forgets to come.
We give you flowers
But it's too late.
We should have given them
To you before.
We write messages,
Not for you, but for ourselves,
To finally fix in our minds
How we felt about you.
Sometimes we lie.
We will remember.
Oh yes, each of us will carry
Into the future
A picture of you,
Something you said
Or something you did.
Most of all,
We will be glad
That we evaded the roulette
And that you were chosen
Rather than us.

Complaint.

Why? Why? Why? Why? Why?
Why did you take away my reason for living?
What good has it done to remove my love?
Who wins? Who benefits? Who cares,
Except I who must now live alone,
Chased by memories, waking each morning
To the dawning realisation that
The rest of my life will be lonely?

Why not take somebody else?
Why didn't you take me,
Or that bad-tempered woman on the corner,
Or a truly wicked person?
Why him? What did he do to deserve it?
He hadn't even finished his boat.
Now it'll sit there, forever half-made,
A reminder of a life cut short.

Why?

Everywhere

I'll play you in my music and
I'll hear you in the choir.
I'll know you are beside me when
I sit down by the fire.
I'll feel you in the morning chill
Before my eyes awake,
And kiss you in my deepest dreams
Before the grey daybreak.

I'll see you every time I look
Inside my poetry pages,
And in the text of every book.
Our love is old as ages.
I'll sense you in the water as
The craft slide gently by.
I'll smell your lovely fragrance.
I'll hold you when I cry.

I'll call you in my nightmares.
I'll taste you in my cheese.
I'll hear your voice a-drifting like
A breath across the seas.
Forever I will have you, though
I know you've gone away.
Your memory still lingers and
You're with me every day.

The Vase of Life

Come walk with me
In the garden of remembrance!
Together we will harvest
Blooms to remind us
Of lovely times together.
Roses, Lavender, Lily of the valley.
Let's place them in the vase of life
And keep them forever.

Soldiering On

You laid down your life for your country
And we are incredibly proud
That you did so along with your comrades,
'Mid the sound of the battle so loud
But sometimes at night when I'm wakeful
And in moonlight your medals are shining,
I know that I miss you so dearly.
For the rest of my life I'll be pining.
Your children will not know a parent,
Your face from the frame always lost,
The ultimate sacrifice given,
And we must bear ever the cost.

Still

We waited with bated breath for you to cry.
Many months of anticipation,
But you were so still.
A hush in the delivery room.
Nervous glances above taut masks.
We dared not ask "Is everything alright?"
A gentle hand, a sad tilt of the head,
And we knew.
We miss you still.

Love's Shadow

Little friend,
You were the rainbow in my heart,
The joy in every morning,
And my soul mate.
Your shadow follows me everywhere
And the echoes of your sighs
Reverberate in my head,
In the day and in the silence of the night.
Sleep well, my darling,
Knowing that my life was better
Because you shared it with me.

The Dark Valley

In the darkness of the valley
Where the day and night are one,
Where the running river murmurs,
Golden tinged from the setting sun,
Where the deer are lying hidden
Among the shadows fading fast,
Where the blackbird sings a solo,
A solemn echo from the past,
Here at peace the world is resting,
Waiting for the velvet sky
To roll across the distant mirage
Heralding that night is nigh.

Evening stars are softly peeping,
Pale as the daisy's sleepy eye.
Gentle zephyrs rustle calmly,
Wings of birds that homeward fly.
As autumn caresses all her children
With a mother's tender hand,
The joy and hope of a new tomorrow
Sweep across the still, quiet land.

Blue Glass

Sunlight streams through blue glass plate,
Casting blue light pools,
Still and deep, as now you sleep.
Your glassware shines like jewels.

On duller days, through autumn haze,
The blue glass cheers my day
And I recall the years we all
Shared, with every ray.

What were your thoughts when gazing on
Your cobalt blue collection,
Alone in your room, in winter gloom,
A time for life's reflection?

I miss your voice on the telephone,
Your lovely sense of humour,
Compassionate ear, wisdom clear
And delight in a family rumour!

We sprinkled ashes on a bitter day
And pretty petals scattered.
It's very true, that wasn't you.
Your life was all that mattered.

I see your smile in that inner eye.
I hear your voice in my dreams,
And you are with me every day
While your blue glass gently gleams.

Bitter Grief

You were never an easy person.
Believe me, how I tried
To reach you. No success though.
I went straight home and cried.
Nothing seemed to please you.
I did my very best,
But something in your make-up
Fouled my useless quest.
I felt you didn't love me.
You always said you did
No matter how I struggled,
To do as I was bid.
I wish that I could grieve more.
I cared so very much.
How I longed for daily,
Your tender, loving touch.
A lifetime full of wishing,
For what could never be,
And now you've quietly left us
With scant propriety.
I look around your bedroom.
Nothing left to show
For all those wasted years.
At last you had to go.
Suffused with my sorrow
And wrapped up in my grief,
I have to say "Goodbye" now,
With a sigh of quiet relief.

Life's Rich Carpet

One door opens and another closes.
It is true, one supposes,
Life is but an endless stream
Of people who, as in a dream,
Come and go from year to year,
Daring one to hold them dear.
Relationships bloom and flower.
Their contents change from hour to hour.
Once a friendship has begun,
Its dallying course will blithely run
'Til circumstances change the rules.
The peak is past. The friendship cools.

A broken marriage or death of those
We hold most dear, will, I suppose,
Change the way we feel t'ward all
Who touch our lives through duty's call,
But each encounter gives and takes,
And life's rich carpet duly makes.
I will not grieve or sadly mourn
For those who pass, or feel forlorn,
But gladly live again and see
The days we spent so happily.
The past is gone, a dying rose.
The future waits and so, here goes…

Seasons

There's a strange sort of mixture
of grief and relief,
For your struggle was painful and long,
And though we're all grieving
And touched by your leaving,
It's sad but you've sung your last song.

We'd have liked you to stay for
sunshine in spring
And maybe next summer's sweet heat,
But your strength ebbed away
At the end of the day
With the sound of your heart's final beat.

Perhaps you'd have made it
to Autumn's full colour
And witnessed the leaves' final splendour,
Rather than paling
And bitterly failing,
In spite of the caring so tender.

To have frolicked through winter
with snowflakes and frost,
Fog in the park and white view,
To have seen shining ice
Would have been nice,
But not the right pathway for you.

For your seasons had all been
accounted,
Your balance of days run away.
So we say, with regret,
We will never forget
And carry you with us each day.

Sunset

When sunset slides behind the hill
And everything on Earth seems still,
When blackbirds sing their last refrain
We celebrate the world again:
Rebirth, renewal, spring, December.
In your name we will remember
All the lovely things we shared,
Knowing surely that you dared
To walk the walk and meet the needs
With acts of kindness, loving deeds,
Little thoughts and words sublime,
Giving others precious time.
So leave us now with love so kissed
And know forever, you'll be missed.

Your Room

I go into your room each day
And start to dust around,
Trying to avoid your cot
That sad and empty stands,
And I recall a tragic dawn
When I found you there,
So quiet like silent, virgin snow
On gently rolling lands.
I took you in my hungry arms,
Thought you were not well.
No warmth returned to greet my love,
My frantic, close embrace.
I held you to me snugly, then
Sniffed your darling skin,
And cast one pensive, frightened glance
At your placid, milk-white face,
That told me all our dreams were dashed.
Hope then drained away,
But, desolate, I dust your room.
I dust your room each day.

Moving On

Hello. It's me.
I've popped into your memory.
Don't be sad!
Instead, be rather glad!
It's O.K.
You haven't thought of me today.
That is how
It's meant to be right now.
Please, no tears!
Images fade with passing years.
I need
You to live on and heed
My advice.
I shouldn't have to say this twice.
Enjoy days,
Happy in lots of ways!
Move on,
Knowing always that I've gone
But I'll be,
Although you can't see me,
In your heart.
We're never really far apart.
Missing you.
Remember I love you too,
........but get on with your life!